No.4 2022

The Kenya

SOCIALIST

Left Views on Elections Under Capitalism

- TO PARTICIPATE OR NOT TO PARTICIPATE
- THE BALLOT OR THE BULLET?
- EDUCATING PEOPLE ABOUT CAPITALISM AND SOCIALISM

Repression & Resistance in Kenya. Part 2: Illustrations

The Kenya Socialist is published by Vita Books, Nairobi, Kenya.
Editors: Shiraz Durrani and Kimani Waweru
February 2022

Uni.Way House, Second Floor, University Way
Next to Lilian Towers Hotel
P.O. Box 62501-00200
Nairobi
Kenya
info.vitabkske@gmail.com
http://vitabooks.co.ke

The Kenya Socialist aims to encourage free flow of information, knowledge and discussion which can lead to a better understanding of socialism. It will seek to:

- Promote socialist ideas, experiences and world outlook
- Increase awareness of classes, class contradictions and class struggles in Kenya, both historical and current
- Expose the damage done by capitalism and imperialism in Kenya and Africa
- Offer solidarity to working class, peasants and other working people and communities in their struggles for equality and justice
- Promote internationalism and work in solidarity with people in Africa and around the world in their resistance to imperialism
- Make explicit the politics of information and communication as tools of repression and also of resistance in Kenya

The Kenya Socialist welcomes submission of relevant articles (normally up to 5,000 words) - send to The Editors at info.vitabkske@gmail.com. The Editors reserve the right not to publish.

The Kenya Socialist is available at: http://vitabooks.co.ke/the-kenya-socialist/
Paper copies are available at Ukombozi Library and from African Books Collective (ABC)
https://www.africanbookscollective.com/publishers/vita-books

ISBN 978-9914-9921-4-4

Cover Photo Illustration Credit: Inquiries Journal

C
O
N
T
E
N
T
S

Editorial: Voting under Capitalism

Kimani Waweru

In the coming months, Kenyan voters will head to the ballot boxes to vote for candidates of their choice. This is a ritual that Kenyans are used to, every five years. Since independence, the country has conducted numerous elections but, as in other capitalists' countries, these elections have always been dominated by the capitalists who happen to control the state. The majority of people have been influenced by ruling class propaganda into believing that voting either of the ruling class candidates will better their lives. This scenario has made people find themselves choosing the candidates of the oppressing class, as Karl Marx said, to repress them: 'The oppressed are allowed once every few years to decide which particular representatives of the oppressing class are to represent and repress them'. Many on the Left, due to opportunism or lack of ideological clarity, find themselves joining the bandwagon and come up with all manner of justification for participating in bourgeoisie elections. A majority of them theorising and quote great revolutionaries like Lenin out of context. Theory is meaningless without practice. And though the Kenyan Left is perhaps strong in theory, it is weak in practice and criticism. Without these, there can be no socialism. These leftist intellectuals and pseudo socialists are in effect champions of capitalism and make it easy for the ruling class to discredit socialism. It is against this background that we dedicate this issue to elections in Kenya.

This issue has four papers that were presented during an ideological seminar on bourgeois elections held at the Kenya National Theatre on 28th July 2021. The seminar was organized by Ukombozi Library, Revolutionary Socialist League (RSL), Women in Social Justice Centers, All African People's Revolutionary Party, Vita Books and the Communist Party of Kenya (CPK). The seminar discussed the role and position of the left in bourgeois elections in Kenya. Some argued that there is a need for the Left to participate in the elections while others argued that based on the real situation, it would be unwise for the Left to participate. It was however noted that the Left is not always against participating in bourgeois elections but the participation has to be guided by concrete conditions of the situation. There are situations where elections can betray the working-class cause and others when it can ripen the revolutionary conditions.

The first article is by Ezra Otieno who argues that any leftist party which wants to participate in elections should be driven by the ideological leanings of the masses. He says that since the majority of people are still not ideologically clear and class-conscious, the duty of the left is to conduct political education with as many people as possible until such time as when subjective and objective conditions are realized. He argues that participation in elections without factoring in these points will be an act of opportunism.

Sobukwe Shukura, a member of the All-African People's Revolutionary Party (AAPRP), argued that the left should use elections as a tactic and a means in a strategical process toward getting power. He gives a brief history of USA elections to show how sometimes it is challenging for a Left party to make an impact in a bourgeois election. He argues that Left parties, as well as individuals, should use elections as a tool to advance people's democracy, not only at elections but at other times too.

Kimani Waweru shows how elections since flag independence in Kenya have been dominated by the rich, making it hard for ordinary citizens to win any elections unless they align with the rich. He argues that the left parties need to hasten the revolutionary moment when it will be easy for the masses to turn against the pro-imperialist parties and embrace progressive political parties.

Zarina Patel and Zahid Rajan, in a joint article, counter the argument by some left parties to justify their participation in elections. They argue that the Kenya Left has no mass base it can rely on. The Kenya Parliament, they argue, is reactionary as seen in how it votes on crucial bills, among them the two third gender rule. They emphasise that the solution lies in studying theory and adapting it to the socio-politico-economic realities. By doing so, the Left would be in a better position to devise new methods of struggle to break through the exploitative system that Kenyans live under.

Kinuthia Ndungu, a Community Organizer and a member of the Communist Party of Kenya (CPK), argues that left parties and individuals in Kenya need to participate in elections. He argues that elections should be used as temporary vehicle to reach the masses and not a substitute for building a revolutionary vanguard. It is because of this reason, he explained, that the CPK will field candidates in the 2022 General Elections. If elected, the Party members will work towards instituting many progressive reforms within the current capitalist system so as to improve the welfare of the exploited and oppressed people. However, the Party will continue to advance the class struggle led by workers and their allies.

David Bii in his article on education shows how socialism has remained relevant even with all the attacks from the ruling class. He argues that there is need to empower the masses via political education in an effort to counter ruling class misinformation about socialism.

Lastly, we present Part 2 of 'Kenya: Repression and Resistance from Colony to Neo-colony 1948–1990' which was first published in the issue No. 3 of TKS (2021) Part 2 carries selected documents, photos and illustrations of resistance.

Our revolution is not a public-speaking tournament. Our revolution is not a battle of fine phrases. Our revolution is not simply for spouting slogans that are no more than signals used by manipulators trying to use them as catchwords, as codewords, as a foil for their own display. Our revolution is, and should continue to be, the collective effort of revolutionaries to transform reality, to improve the concrete situation of the masses of our country.

Thomas Sankara

A newspaper is not only a collective propagandist and a collective agitator, it is also a collective organiser.

Left view on Elections

Ezra Otieno is an organizer and a member of the Central Committee of the Revolutionary Socialist League (RSL) in Kenya. He is also a member of Ukombozi Library

There is a prevalent misconception that Marxism is solely concerned with economics. It is undeniably true that Marxists believe that society's economic relations form its foundation, and that you can't understand the dynamics of a particular society unless you understand its underlying relations of production and class. "What distinguishes the various economic formations of society," Marx wrote in Capital, "is the manner in which…surplus labor is extorted from the immediate producer, the worker."

Arguments among the Kenyan left regarding participation in parliamentary elections have rekindled great interest on the topic of bourgeoisie elections to the left worldwide. The dilemma facing the Kenyan left is an appropriate point for engaging with the radical thoughts of Vladimir Lenin on the meaning of participating in parliamentary elections. This paper discusses his view of the link between strategy and tactics in parliamentary elections. The paper also summarizes attempts to decipher the relevance of Lenin's arguments on parliamentary elections.

To start with, the state is a crucial component of the superstructure as it includes not only coercive agencies and official bureaucracies, but also legislative and executive bodies that switch hands between rival political parties, at least in systems where elections are held. Even in the most democratic form of the state, Engels defined the modern state as "the institution which the ruling classes—landowners and capitalists—have constructed for themselves in order to safeguard their social advantages. As a result, the working class must become involved in politics. To accomplish liberation, it must form its own autonomous political party."

In a resolution in 1871 written for the International Workingmen's Association's London convention, Karl Marx argued that the "only way to guarantee the success of the social revolution and its ultimate end—the abolition of classes, the working class must create a party that is different from, and hostile to, the former parties formed by the propertied classes."

The workers' party must never be the tag tail of any bourgeois party; it must be autonomous, with its own aims and strategies. Perceptions of many people on politics are often shared around the restrictive boundaries of the multi-party system. Politics are viewed as the domain of politicians that have little to do with 'us' and by 'us' of the working class.

In the Kenyan context, just like in other capitalist systems in the world, any progressive party must be driven by the masses. Participation in elections by leftists must be informed by the ideological leanings of the masses. In Kenya, where a large number of people are still not ideologically conscious, the duty of every revolutionary is to conduct political education with as many people as possible until such a time when subjective and objective conditions are realized. Radical political education would entail determining the tactics and strategies to be used to capture state power. Until then, the mission of any serious left party is to conduct radical political education among the masses.

Other sections of the left movement use the term "infiltration", meaning joining bourgeoisie institutions, such as Parliaments, and attempting to change them from within. Looking at the current conditions in Kenya, it would be practically impossible to bring change this way given the tribal inclinations of our political parties. Any progressive party would have to stoop to the level of these parties and mobilize along tribal lines and as argued earlier, the masses that are not yet politically conscious will treat this party as the usual liberal party. We can also learn from the experiences of "progressive" comrades who have vied for political seats and how they conformed to the norms of the capitalist system and did little or nothing at all to change the material conditions of the masses. These comrades seem opportunistic as they engaged in bourgeoisie elections without a critical analysis of the ideological levels and material conditions of the people.

Political parties that have ruled Kenya since independence have championed bourgeoisie interests at the expense of the masses, consequently alienating them. It is no wonder that most people do not take elections seriously. For many people, elections are chances to "eat" from the competing politicians. When the masses engage in politics, they realize that no party appears to be working in their best interests. Most liberal parties are meant to safeguard the interests of those referred to as the "captains of industry", that is, bankers, industrialists, merchants, investors, and other corporate bigwigs. People who desire to bring genuine and meaningful social change need to question themselves constantly on the meaning of elections. If elections are about the government, adopting policies that benefit businesses must be for the benefit of the working class. Regardless of the party that is in power, the massive machinery that runs the state is inextricably linked to commercial interests that are held by the revolving doors of lobbyists, attorneys, and the so-called "regulatory" officials who alternate between the state and private sectors.

In my opinion, under no circumstance should a truly leftist party take part in bourgeoisie elections given the current conditions in the country. Revolutionaries can only take part in elections as a tactic when they are certain that the masses are politically conscious to understand the limits of bourgeoisie elections. Until then, engagement in radical political education should be the number one priority of our party.

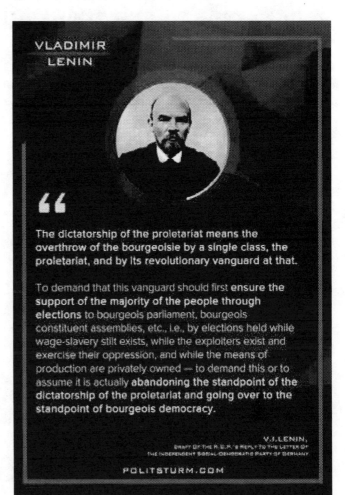

VLADIMIR LENIN

" The dictatorship of the proletariat means the overthrow of the bourgeoisie by a single class, the proletariat, and by its revolutionary vanguard at that.

To demand that this vanguard should first **ensure the support of the majority of the people through elections** to bourgeois parliament, bourgeois constituent assemblies, etc., i.e., by elections held while wage-slavery still exists, while the exploiters exist and exercise their oppression, and while the means of production are privately owned — to demand this or to assume it is actually **abandoning the standpoint of the dictatorship of the proletariat and going over to the standpoint of bourgeois democracy.**

V.J.LENIN,
DRAFT OF THE R.C.P.'S REPLY TO THE LETTER OF THE INDEPENDENT SOCIAL-DEMOCRATIC PARTY OF GERMANY

POLITSTURM.COM

You can kill a revolutionary, but you cannot kill a revolution.

— *Fred Hampton* —

AZ QUOTES

Ballot or the Bullet: Revolutionary Change by All Means Necessary

Sobukwe Shukura is a member of The All-African People's Revolutionary Party (AAPRP)

The All-African People's Revolutionary Party (AAPRP) had a slogan in the 70's and the 80's: "Smash the Democratic and Republican Party". We have today a more appropriate line calling for the dismantling of all bourgeoise parties globally. The AAPRP believes these capitalist parties cannot be redeemed. Some have mistakenly understood this to mean the AAPRP is against left participation in elections. Not only is that not true, but the AAPRP has supported many of our revolutionary Pan-African and other Socialist alliances in their bid for power through the electoral process in Guinea Conakry, Guinea Bissau, Azania/South Africa, Brazil, Bolivia, Nicaragua, Venezuela, Zimbabwe etc. The AAPRP is not an electoral party at this stage. We are committed to organizing for Pan-Africanism and bringing together revolutionary African organizations globally in the fight against our common enemy - imperialism.

"We must understand the politics of our community. And we must know what politics is supposed to produce. We must know what (role) politics play in our lives. And until we become politically mature? We will always be misled, lead astray, or deceived, or maneuvered into supporting someone politically, who doesn't (have) the good of our community at heart. So, the political philosophy of Black Nationalism only means that we will have to carry on a political program of reeducation: to open our people's eyes; make us (become) more politically conscious, politically mature; and then we will, whenever we get ready to cast our ballot? That ballot will be cast for a man (person) of the community, who has the good of the community at heart." Malcolm X The Ballot or the Bullet Speech Transcript - Malcolm X - Rev

We are sure with a close examination of Malcolm X's now famous speech "The Ballot or the Bullet" he was clear that the ballot is a tactic not a principle. The ballot is a tactic like armed struggle or non-violent direct action, (strikes, marches, sit-ins, etc.). Malcolm X said 'by any means necessary' in his 1964 speech given at the founding of the Organization of Afro-American Unity. We might say today by "All Means Necessary". Kwame Ture and other members of The Student Non-Violent Coordinating Committee (SNCC) members said often that Martin Luther King and the Southern Christian Leadership Council saw non-violence as a principle and not a tactic ("Eyes On Prize Interviews" Judy Richarson's Question 27 to Kwame Ture). If you see non-violence or violence, armed struggle or electoral politics as principles they become ends in themselves and not merely means to an end. Let me be clear here that the All-African People's Revolutionary Party sees voting and electoral politics as a tactic and a means in a strategical process toward power. All strategy and tactics of any political party or formation must be guided by an ideology leading to clear objectives. That objective for the AAPRP is: One unified Socialist Africa. The objective of those in power is to stay in power, all others are seeking to either share or seize power. The objective of Neo-colonial, Settler and Capitalist parties is to maintain power. Therefore, all their organizational energies are used in this manner. Even the way they organize elections and election processes are designed for them to stay in power.

"Revolution is a science. It is not about feelings or sentimentality but what we call a dialectical & historical analysis of history. It requires having clearly defined goals and objectives based on the scientific analysis of the strengths and weaknesses of the people and the enemy. It is about developing and implementing a winning strategy and making adjustments when strategies fail and/or become obsolete." "Pan-Africanism and International Solidarity: Two Complementary Elements of the A-APRP" AAPRP-International.org

The bourgeoise capitalist democratic state is designed to keep capitalism in power. Since capitalism represents a minority of the population and not the people's interests, the only way it can stay in power is by keeping the people divided and powerless. In the first so-called modern democracies like the United States in 1776, only rich white land owners could vote. Every other sector of the society including Africans, workers and women got the vote by shedding their blood in the streets. Today after over almost 200 years, U.S. Settler Capitalism uses white supremist strategies to divide the electorate and suppress the vote. For working class people in the U.S. there is no mass party that represents either their economic interest or principally their social interest. The questions of race, gender, religion are used to mobilize the people but not to organize them. Africans (people of African descent) in the U.S. fought and died for the right to vote in the U.S. The Student Non-Violent Coordinating Committee (SNCC) workers, working in the voting campaigns in the Southern United States saw that the Civil Rights movement had no strategy on how to use the vote for gaining political power beyond increasing Africans in the U.S. with the vote numerically, to just vote and elect more "Black People" to the same racist capitalist system. From then up to now, there are only the two, racist settler-capitalist parties, the democrats and the republicans, that have locked down the electoral process. The young SNCC workers helped to form alternative parties including the "Mississippi Freedom Democratic Party" and "Lowndes County Freedom Party (Black Panther Party)" in the sixties. The "Black Panther Party", known for its symbol, was able to register and increase people of African descent voting numbers in their local area. The Mississippi Freedom Democratic Party (MFDP) fielded a slate of alternative delegates to the Democratic Convention and challenged the all-white slate that was chosen without the participation of the African (Black) population. The Democratic Party refused MFDP delegates and offered them only one seat which MFDP refused. Ideologically though left of the Settler-regime, neither of these formations had socialist ideologies and those forces from them who didn't move on to left organizations, became Democrats. Almost 90 percent of the African elected officials belong to the democratic party. Although some reforms have been made, the African people have very little power in the Democratic Party per their numbers. Indeed, the numerically smaller Zionist lobby yields much more power than Africans in the Democratic Party. The call for Black Power, a slogan raised by SNCC, sparked an important debate over the use of the vote as a tactic for electoral influence verses using it to gain political power. Using the vote to gain political power requires a revolutionary political party or front of parties with a mass character, organizing workers, women, youth, peasants, etc.

The socialist and communist parties in the U.S. have only been elected as mayors, congressmen, senators and so forth in their individual capacity. The power of Communists in the United States was gutted in the 1940's under the "McCarthy Internal Security Act" that expelled communists from the industrial unions. The U.S. Unions of today are largely aligned to the Democratic Party and their Capitalist and Imperialist foreign policies. The closest leftist ever to becoming a U.S. President was Social Democrat, Bernie Sanders, who ran as a Democrat. Today the left organizations have no collective electoral front or collective strategy and individually these Parties have never gotten more than 3% of the vote.

We make these observations because of the undue influence the bourgeois form of so called "democratic elections" dominate the discourse of the neo-colonial state in Africa and the world. These capitalist elections promote form over essence, the individual over the collective and a horse race instead of the battle of ideas. There is in essence a one-party state in the U.S., Australia and Israel in the sense that the major competing parties support setter-capitalism. The neo-colonial states in Africa were formed by collusion with local opportunist elites and coercive forces from imperialist states. Imperialism will support multiparty, one party, or an autocratic state if it meets its interests, for example by their historical support of the one-party state in Kenya and now the multi-party state in Kenya. History actually shows that for the oppressed, a socialist one party-state has advanced the people's interest more rapidly than the multi-party model. Russia, China, Ghana, Cuba, Guinea Conakry and Guinea Bissau advanced in all the social fields for instance education, health care as well as women's and worker's rights under a one-party state. Multi-Partyism in Africa took two forms: First, people's defense against neo-colonial capitalist one-party states and semi-feudal regimes, and secondly by the imperialist imposed multi-partyism to destroy the power of one-party socialist governments and to retard cohesion among ethnic groups and other social strata. Guinea Conakry under the African Democratic Party of Guinea (PDG) banned parties based on ethnicity or religion. This is to point out that in neo-colonial and former colonial states in general and in Africa in particular, we are fighting both internal contradictions micro-nationalisms, semi-feudal traditions and external contradictions of foreign finance (IMF, Barclays Bank, Foreign/Settler controlled industries and land), and military apparatuses that occupy the state (AFRICOM, NATO, Israel Security Firms).

There are many examples of left fronts formed

to take power through electoral politics like Chile, Venezuela, Brazil, some formed during the revolutionary process and others after the execution of an armed struggle in the context of Algeria, Tanzania, Cuba. There are parties that came to power in Africa using elections that then proceeded to embark on building socialist societies after taking power including Ghana and Guinea Conakry etc. The critical process for Left participation, we reiterate here, is that there must be a revolutionary strategy. What are the forces in tension? Is the left unified? Are the left parties or fronts unified around a common ideology or platform? If the state is neo-colonial, are there nationalist parties that want to free the state from foreign economic domination? Is there a land question? What is the strength of labor? What is the strength of women and youth movements and organizations? Do you have more chances of victory on the local level? Are there seats on the national level? Is this a campaign of exposure for your organization and your platform? Most of all, can you build a left party/front that can distinguish itself ideologically and politically from the ruling class agenda? Many Left powers have simply been absorbed by the state. The current election in Kenya is largely a collaboration between the same ruling elites. The 2022 election started in Kenya in 2018 and to date there is no Left candidate or coalition built yet capable of changing the old guard on the presidential or national level. The Communist Party Kenya recently announced their decision to form a coalition with several coast parties and made overtures with other like-minded parties. There is some value in this even if the effort yields few electoral votes in the 2022 election. The bigger challenge is building a nationwide left people-centered coalition that is at a minimum anti-neo-colonial and anti-patriarchal. The Revolutionary Pan-Africanist Kwame Nkrumah said in a speech at the Organization of African Unity in 1963 the following about national independence.

"On this continent, it has not taken us long to discover that the struggle against colonialism does not end with the attainment of national independence. Independence is only the prelude to a new and more involved struggle for the right to conduct our own economic and social affairs; to construct our society according to our aspirations, unhampered by crushing and humiliating neo-colonialist controls and interference." Kwame Nkrumah (Read Entire 1963 OAU Speech)

Revolutionary Pan-Africanist and socialist internationalists must look at elections as a tool to advance people's democracy; popular democracy that strengthens mass participation not only in elections but participation in the political life of the society. Their goal must again be organization not just mobilization. There must be popular political education like in Venezuela around the constitution for instance, while recruiting and increasing ideologically trained cadre in the party/parties. Amilcar Cabral said, one of the greatest weaknesses of national liberation parties and organizations has been the lack of constant ideological training. Revolutionaries must also be honest about their own strength and the strength of the other political forces before competing for office. Sometimes a campaign against neo-colonial elections can be just as effective in organizing the people's political power. For revolutionaries, every election in Africa and the world is our concern because each election either advances, retards or supports the current status in the fight against imperialism. Africa is under neo-colonialism today; neo-colonialism is imperialism and no state alone can defeat imperialism. Summarily one ethic group or sector cannot defeat a neo-colonial state. Achieving Africa's sovereignty is based on our struggle for pan-African working-class organization, locally, continentally and internationally. Many errors have been made by the Left in our election strategies emerging from colonialism.

The mass parties in Azania/South Africa gives us a good example here. The national liberation parities in Southern Africa particularly Azania/Southern Africa had a mass character bringing together workers, youth, women and a revolutionary Pan-African/Socialist intelligentsia. They waged political struggle using armed struggle, strikes and marches, garnering Pan-African and other international support. The freedom fighters from the Southern African Region had support bases throughout the continent from Ghana and Guinea Conakry to Libya and Tanzania and received material from the OAU African Liberation Committee. The Cubans sent tens of thousands of troops to Angola alone. Liberated states like Guinea Bissau Angola, Mozambique, and Zimbabwe fought together against the remaining Settler-Regime in Azania/South Africa. The three major liberation forces of the African National Congress (ANC), Pan-Africanist Congress of Azania and Azanian People's Organization could not achieve a revolutionary front before going into the elections in 1994. This lack of an African Left front gave more negotiating power to the minority settler-class parties supported by global capital. The ANC negotiated away three of their main political positions before the elections. 1) They would not disarm until liberation was won; 2) The resources would be nationalized and 3) the elections would be based on one person one vote. The ANC was the majority party in 1994 and still is but other parties are gaining ground like the left leaning "Economic Freedom Party" and the right "National Alliance Party". There is a growing class struggle inside and out of the ANC coalition. Congress of South African Trade Unions (COSATU) expelled the National Union of Metal Workers of South Africa (NUMSA) from the trade union federation, sparking formation of Socialist Revolutionary Workers Party (SRWP). There is renewed energy among the youth calling for more socialist policies. The pressure to address land reclamation, neo-colonial corruption and white settler-capitalism (who controls 70% of capital in South Africa) is driving the discussion. If the left parties consolidated in Azania/South Africa it would be a major blow to imperialism on the continent.

I note four things in conclusion:
1) Left Parties need a common electoral strategy.
2) Left parties need a national coalition/front of workers, women and youth
3) Left parties need a developed propaganda machine capable of waging ideological struggle nationally and internationally
4) Left forces in Africa have to unite organizationally across the continent building an "All-African Committee for Political Coordination" leading to a continental wide socialist political party.

"Anytime you throw your weight behind a political party that controls two-thirds of the government, and that Party can't keep the promise that it made to you during election time, and you're dumb enough to walk around continuing to identify yourself with that Party, you're not only a chump, but you're a traitor to your race. ...You put them first, and they put you last, 'cause you're a chump, a political chump."
- Malcolm X, speeches

The Reality of *Bwanyenye or Bourgeoisie* Elections - To Participate or not to Participate

Kimani Waweru

In every country, the election of people to political positions presents an opportunity to the citizenry to choose those who can tackle their prevailing issues. Most countries in the world undergo this process at a specified interval. Due to the privileges associated with political offices in capitalist countries, candidates scramble for votes from electorates with exaggerated promises. Once elected, most of the politicians ignore their promises and concentrate on self-aggrandizement. They normally use their positions to influence the award of state contracts to people they have connections with or to extort bribes from those they award contracts to.

It is too costly to vie for elective positions in Kenya and this is one of the reasons elections are dominated by the wealthy. It becomes extremely difficult for an ordinary citizen, however popular, to win an election unless they pay homage to political parties run and controlled by the ruling class. Upon being elected, their allegiance goes to the bwanyenye (bourgeois) party rather than to those who elected him. In Kenya, major political parties are usually controlled by the bwanyenye class (powerful and rich people) imbued with the ideology of capitalism. These intrigues are not apparent to ordinary citizens due to the tight control of the means of communication (media) by the same class. These bwanyenye parties deceive the masses by articulating issues affecting working people and promising to solve their problems. Once in power, they renege on their promises which are contrary to their true class interests and replace them with capitalistic policies geared towards acquisition of wealth at the expense of the poor.

In the recent past, key leaders and the lieutenants of these political parties have been traversing the country deceiving Kenyans by telling them what they want to hear and not necessarily what they can do for them. The politicians dwell on attacking their fellow bwanyenye opponents from other parties, implying they are better than them. Ironically, their rallies are well attended by the oppressed and suffering Kenyans who innocently believe them in the hope that their lives will be easy upon electing either of the rival politicians.

The reality of Kenyan elections over the years has been the dominance of elites and the wealthy, most of who owe allegiance to the former colonialists. It is therefore not surprising to see that all Kenyan general elections have over the years been backed by western imperialists countries. They make sure that the competing political parties, especially the bigger ones, share the capitalistic ideology of individualism, stealing wealth from workers and peasants, and promotion of antipeople neoliberal policies. Where there is no leftist or pro-people party or it is weak and its ideologies unknown to the people, like in Kenya, the imperialists feel strong enough to dictate to the bwanyenye political parties on how to conduct their affairs. These bwanyenye parties, on the other hand, are not homogeneous; some are liberal, right wing, centre right, social democrats while others pose as leftist but when push comes shove, they jump to petty bougeosis tendencies. It is no wonder that one finds members of such pseudo leftist parties asking voters to vote for them and vote for their affiliated bourgeosis presidential candidate especially when they are contesting in areas where a certain presidential candidate is popular. The lack of strong leftist party makes the imperialists choose among the bourgeoises parties; the one that accommodates their interests the most. Once they choose one, the other bwanyenye parties which are not favored normally castigate the imperialists, telling Kenyans that their problems cannot be tackled by the western/ foreign countries as if they would not have worked with the imperialists had they been chosen instead.

In case a socialist party gains strength and people understand its ideology and thereby threatens the bwanyenye parties, the imperialists mobilize all the bwanyenye parties irrespective of their stand and make them end their differences by uniting them by all means against such a leftist party. This tactic was exercised very well in Nicaragua when all rightist parties were forced to support one candidate (Violeta Chamora) against Sandinista candidate (Daniel Ortega) in the1990 general elections. This conspiracy saw Violeta emerge the victor.

In 2017 general elections when bwanyenye political parties i.e. ODM, Jubilee, Wiper, ANC and Ford Kenya were competing, the imperialists did not interference apart since they knew that either camp will side with them upon taking power. Another thing one needs to understand is that even if imperialist countries share the same ideology, they compete among themselves for the wealth in the countries of the South since this is a rule of capitalism. They work together on some fundamentals but differ on non-fundamentals. The contradiction between the USA and UK is not a fundamental one while that between the Kenyan people and the comprador regime which is in service of the imperialists is a fundamental one. Therefore, if the two imperialist countries differ, Kenyan people should not assume that they are not together on fundamental issues affecting our people.

What is to be done?

Some leftist individuals in Kenya have over the years boycotted general elections citing lack of changes in the regime as reasons for refraining. Others have claimed that since the regime is controlled by the bwanyenye parties it would be hard for them to make any impact. Yet another group, due to either opportunism and/or ideological weaknesses which renders them unable to understand that the struggle for genuine change takes long time, get tired and opt to join bwanyenye politics. They justify their opportunistic move by arguing that for one to change the regime, one has to be inside it. Upon election, some of these people get disillusioned once they realize that they cannot change a neocolonial state from within, as any positive initiative is frustrated. Some end up joining the bandwagon of other MPs in looting and corrupting the country, thus enriching themselves.

The issue of progressive or leftist individuals participating in bwanyenye election is one which needs to be debated seriously since it is complex. In some cases, there is a need for participating while in others it may not be wise. For one to make the right choice, a scientific analysis of the situation has to be undertaken. The analysis should look at the forces behind the bwanyenye regime and also the strength of the alternative force (leftist party). The needs of the poor masses (workers, peasants etc.) should also be considered since one is participating in elections to help them achieve their goals. If such participation will boost the struggle for the people against neocolonial regime and ripen the revolutionary situation, then doing so will be right. But if nothing will be achieved and instead the neocolonial regime will take advantage in entrenching itself and confusing the masses, then participation will

be a betrayal of the revolutionary struggle and the masses. But the most important point to note is that one needs to contest through a socialist party. It is the party that should do the analysis and decide whether it is appropriate to contest.

In Kenya, like in many countries in the South, the objective conditions for revolution are ripe but the catalyst (a revolutionary party) is weak. This has led to subjective conditions or the consciousness of the masses being very low. In such a situation, the progressive patriots should continue organizing and exposing the contradiction within the capitalist society and exposing the political bankruptcy of the neocolonial state through a Marxist-Leninist-Maoist party. They should continue to advocate for the immediate needs of the masses in a situation in which the neocolonial state does not implement measures such as the nationalization of public utilities, provision of free medical care, resettling of landless people, free and compulsory education, subsidizing basic commodities such as food and the provision of housing, among others. In so doing, they will be in a good position to win the masses to their side and expose the deception of the bwanyenye political parties. This act should be waged in a determined manner knowing very well that it is only by doing so that the battle will be won. This will contribute to hastening the revolutionary moment whereby it will be easy for the masses to turn against the pro-imperialist parties and embrace the socialist political party. We should also be aware that the reactionary forces will not just wait and let things turn to the advantage of the socialist party. They will use the state machinery which they control to hamper any move that could make them lose power. But if the party cadres are ideologically equipped with a scientific theory - such as Marxism-Leninism-Maoism (MLM) - to demystify the capitalist system which oppresses and exploits our people, and to illuminate the path to be used in liberating themselves, they will be able to overcome such challenges and lead the party to victory.

Last, I want to conclude by reading out a passage from Bob Avakian, the Chairman of Revolutionary Communist party of USA:

> "The capitalists control the system of elections, and every other dominant institution, in this country. Voting under this system, for either the existing bourgeoisis parties, is voting for ruling

class parties who are determined to keep this system going, despite the terrible cost to the masses of humanity, and even with the very real threat this poses to the existence of humanity.

No matter what promises these politicians make—and no matter what schemes people try to come up with to make things more "just" or "equal" under this system—none of this can change the basic nature of this system and the way it has to operate because of its very nature.

The relations of exploitation and oppression that are built into this system are enforced through its institutions of official power and violence— the parliament and the presidency, the courts, and especially the police and the military."

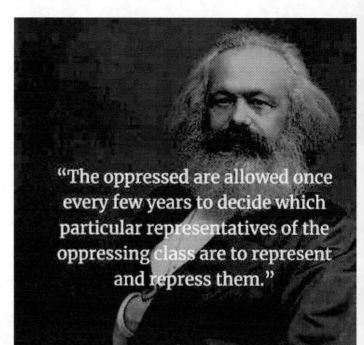

"The oppressed are allowed once every few years to decide which particular representatives of the oppressing class are to represent and repress them."

Karl Marx

> "
>
> # The liberal bourgeoisie grant reforms with one hand,
>
> and with the other **always take them back**, reduce them to nought, use them to enslave the workers, to divide them into separate groups and **perpetuate wage-slavery.**
>
> **V. I. Lenin**
> "Marxism and Reformism"
>
> US.POLITSTURM.

Should the Left Avoid Parliaments and Elections Altogether?

Kinuthia Ndung'u:

This paper is written as a contribution to the ideological seminar "The Role of the Left and Social Movements in Elections" held at Kenya National Theater, Cheche gallery on 28th July 2021. I pen this modest contribution to highlight my position on the question as we celebrate the reincarnation of Allende in Gabriel Boric's electoral victory in Chile. We also celebrate with Bolivia the victory of MAS party Presidential candidate Luis Arce that culminated in the return of Evo Morales. Both Allende and Evo were democratically elected but overthrown by counter revolutionary violence with the help of US imperialism, ushering in neo-liberal governments. There is a need to acknowledge mistakes made, ascertaining the reasons for them, analyzing the conditions that led up to them and then rectifying errors. History is important in our analysis, those who cannot remember the past are condemned to repeat it.

Can socialists reform the state apparatus of the current system to become a new and better one?

I remind you of Germany in the early 20th century, The Social Democrats were split between reformist who thought they could vote socialism into existence, and revolutionaries like Rosa Luxemburg, who, while valuing reforms, argued that capitalism and democracy were incompatible in the long run. The pamphlet Reform or Revolution, (Luxemburg, 1900), critiqued the reformism of Edward Bernstein who redefined the fundamental character of labour movement as a "democratic social reform party" and not a party of social revolution. Rosa Luxemburg viewed electoralism as a tool to build class consciousness and extract concessions but not to solve the inherent contradictions. Another pamphlet - The Elections to the National Assembly (Luxemburg, 1918) - argues that our participation in elections was primarily to cast out the bourgeoisie and raise the victorious banner of proletarian revolution.

It sounds contradictory to admit the impossibility of building socialism via the electoral path yet contest for electoral positions, right?

Petty bourgeois democrats replaced class struggles with dreams of class harmony, and even pictured socialist transformation in a dreamy fashion. This attitude to the state is a manifestation of the fact that they were sham socialists using neo-socialist phraseology. As socialists, we are opponents of the dictatorship of the bourgeoisie. We must uphold the revolutionary aspects of Marxism and stand against bourgeois reformism. Marx and Engels argued that the class struggle in France had proved that the working class could not simply lay hold of the readymade state machinery and wield it for its own purpose.

The *State and Revolution* (Lenin, 1917) gives a good introduction to the nature of the state and why getting socialism is not simply a question of voting for left parties in an election. In *Theses on the Communist Parties and Parliamentarism* (Second Congress of the Communist International, 1920), Lenin, explaining the reason for us to participate in these elections, noted:

> The argument that parliament is a bourgeois state institution cannot be used against parliamentary struggle. The communist Party does not enter these institutions in order to carry out organic work there, but in order to help the masses break up the state machine and the parliament itself through action…."

Lenin's position is rooted in what Marx and Engels argued before him; that a socialist party should stand for parliamentary elections, not with the primary intention of passing reforms and not for a moment renouncing the revolutionary conquest of power by the proletariat. Our participation in election is therefore a matter of tactic rather than strategy. After the collapse of the 1st international, Engels argued against abstentionism (from elections). He wrote on the need to utilize all forms of struggle and conceive them as an overall strategy for revolution. As for the left organizing in Kenya, it is a correct idea for us to participate in both the parliamentary and extra parliamentary struggle, at both above and below levels. This participation in elections is necessary as a rule, unless in the circumstance where the mood of our masses is rebellious and the objective conditions are ripe for revolution. We should however be careful not to relegate ourselves to a strategy of inheriting the existing rotten state which has proved to be a great waste of time for decades across Africa, Asia and Latin America.

Our participation in bourgeois elections can be a useful tactic, but there are limits to how far we should go down that road. Our participation must always be in the form of the worker's parties. Lenin and his comrades formed the Russian Social Democratic Labour Party to maintain their class independence while espousing socialist ideas to the workers. To spend time supporting any candidate running within any bourgeois political party is an opportunity cost in terms of time that we cannot afford.

The Communist Party of Kenya believes in elections in so far as it is a temporary vehicle to reach the masses and not a substitute for building a revolutionary vanguard. In the pamphlet "Left-Wing" Communism: An Infantile Disorder (Vladimir, 1920), Lenin's underlying argument called on revolutionary socialists to work wherever the masses were to be found. This meant communists had to work with reformist trade unions and also participate in parliamentary elections. He correctly analyzed that the workers had illusions in the parliamentary system and therefore they had to capitalize on that platform to educate the masses in order to enlighten and awaken their consciousness. The pamphlet also spells out electoral alliances forged between the Bolsheviks and bourgeois reactionaries. This was a tactical way of reaching the masses to advance their ideological and political struggle against the opportunist and reformist voices.

Mwandawiro Mghanga, the Chair of the Communist Party of Kenya (CPK), in the article The 2022 National Elections; Kenyans Think Outside the Box (Kwaela News Network, 2019) addressed the question of participation in the coming elections. He noted;

> "To them you from the working class in the box and who tear each other apart in your own ethnicity especially during the elections, as you did in 2007/8 and repeated in 2017, thinking you belong to the same ethnicity with them, they use and dump you in the dust bin of poverty, marginalization and backwardness where you will belong until the next elections

or until and unless you get yourselves out of the box. For to them you in the box are mere elections statistics and voting machines"

He argued that the reactionary politicians have cornered the voters. They use all the means at their disposal, including, but not limited to the press, tribalism, political meetings and all the machinery of propaganda to ensure voters remain permanently fixed in the reactionary box. The people are then forced to decide between corrupt and tribal candidates who hardly think about legislating to really improve conditions of workers. He concludes that the CPK believes in progressive reforms aimed at improving the welfare of the exploited and oppressed as it advances class struggle led by workers and their allies

The Constitution of Kenya 2010 has expanded civil liberties and allows the left to organize overtly. This is an opportunity to fight on all fronts and CPK will therefore field candidates for different positions. In fact, the party has already established a United Political Coalition at the Coast ahead of the 2022 elections. This gives the party a platform to lead debates on issues such as historical land injustices and privatization of the Port of Mombasa, thereby deepening the debate on alternatives to neo-liberalism and capitalism. Our reality is that the masses still believe elections are the only way to bring about a meaningful change. Do we leave these politically activated masses to the hands of reactionary politicians with backward ideas? The coming elections offer CPK a platform to expose the systemic failure of capitalism in Kenya, counter capitalist propaganda, measure our power of organizing and develop class-consciousness among our people.

If CPK is able to capture seats in the coming bourgeois elections, it embarks on reforms –not as a way to socialism, but progressive reforms to make people's lives better. These policies are clearly outlined in the Minimum and Maximum program of the party (Communist Party of Kenya, 2019). The Kenyan Constitution 2010 can be used to institute many progressive reforms within our current capitalist system. As students of history, we are aware that freedom and liberation of our society will ultimately only be realized when the current system of capitalism is replaced by a historically higher, progressive and human socialist system.

References

Luxemburg, R. (1900). Reform or Revolution. London: Militant Publications.

Luxemburg, R. (1918). The Elections to the National Assembly. Random House.

Lenin, V. (1917). The State and Revolution.

Second Congress of the Communist International. (1920). Theses on Communist Parties and Parliamentarism. Saint Petersburg. Retrieved from marxist.org: https://www.marxist.org/history/international/cominterm/2nd-congress/ch08a.htm

Vladimir, L. (1920). Left Wing Communism: An Infantile Disorder. London: Executive Commettee of the Communist International.

Kwaela News Network. (2019, August 12th). Retrieved from kwaela.co.ke: https://kwaela.co.ke/the-2022-national-elections-kenyans-think-outside-the-the-box/amp/

Communist Party of Kenya. (2019). Communist Party of Kenya. Retrieved from communistpartyofkenya.org: https://communistpartyofkenya.org/87-recent-news/235-summary-of-the-minumum-programe-of-the-communist-party-of-kenya-cpk

Democracy cannot consist solely of elections that are nearly always fictitious and managed by rich landowners and professional politicians.

(Che Guevara)

izquotes.com

Before a revolution happens, it is perceived as impossible; after it happens, it is seen as having been inevitable.

— *Rosa Luxemburg* —

AZ QUOTES

Should the Left Participate in the 2022 General Election or Boycott It?

Zarina Patel & Zahid Rajan

I've come to learn that if you want to change the world, you must change people[1] *Shyam Shah*

Topic: Should the left participate in the 2022 general election or boycott it?

Presumed Objective: That electing a few Left-leaning members to Parliament will lead to Parliament upholding the Constitution and ensuring more just and democratic law-making.

Our position: That at this point in time and given the prevailing circumstances, even if we were able to get a few progressive and Leftist members elected to Parliament (which we think unlikely), they would make very little, if any, impact on the present parliamentary modus operandi. So, the question is not: Should we boycott the Election? It is 'Should we, in the present stage of our political organising, even think of participating in a parliamentary election?' We maintain that the time (2 years if not more), resources and energy our small group of radical activists would expend in campaigning would be infinitely better spent building the mass base without which no meaningful change is possible.

In October 2020, in response to this position, the Communist Party of Kenya (CPK) asked us to read Vladimir Lenin's 'Left-Wing' Communism – An Infantile Disorder'. We did so and to summarise: our main argument was that when Lenin wrote this theoretical piece, he did so with the backing of a Socialist Party and a politically advanced mass base. To date we have neither in Kenya. That is not in any way to denigrate the efforts being made to build a left constituency and raise socialist awareness; but to recognise that we are yet very much in our infancy.

1. THE PARTY/ORGANISATION. We are extremely small in numbers and even that minority is organisationally fragmented because, we think, overall, we lack ideological theory and clarity as well as genuine commitment. In short, we have a long way to go before we can apply Lenin's theory re 'Should we participate in Bourgeois Parliaments?'

It is important to note that Lenin did also write that, 'parliamentarism is historically obsolete because a free and fair election can never be held in a capitalist society … but it is politically desirable because of the generally held view by the masses that parliamentary elections are the only route to ensuring democracy'.

This 'political desire' is very true of the Kenyan public which puts its faith in a 'free and fair election' and has no inkling of a possible alternative because, in the absence of any ideological education/exposure, it accepts unquestioningly the imperialist model.

2. THE MASS BASE. We have no mass base to speak of. What we do have in Kenya is masses of suffering wananchi who are thoroughly disgruntled and disillusioned by the ruling class but see no alternative. The latter is emphasised because people have little or no understanding of the workings of the system which oppresses them and a possible alternative. This is hardly surprising given that even in our 'progressive' middle class circles, the word 'capitalism' is hardly ever mentioned or analysed while 'socialism' is grossly mis-used and 'Imperialism' is not even on the horizon. 'Class struggle' more often than not is simply the aspiration to move up the social ladder and escape the grinding inequality.

The reality: We have (and have had) a Parliament which is unashamedly capitalist, sexist, homophobic, self-seeking, corrupt and un-informed. There have always been a few stalwarts who try to swim against the tide but have to invariably toe the line or get over-ruled. The two-thirds gender rule, the issue of salaries and perks, the non-implementation of the Ndungu and TJRC Reports - are just some of the glaring failings of this so-called 'august' house. I am sure we are all in agreement with these facts and need no convincing.

There is another of Lenin's teachings we need to emphasise. He has stated unequivocally that 'the state is a tool of the ruling class'. The state is not neutral – it has a class base and operates on behalf of big capital. It engages several bodies such as the police, the army, the parliament and the media to maintain and sustain its interests and its supremacy. There is no way the oligarchs and their allies will allow any loss of control of this important 'tool'. Elections for them are just a ploy to pacify the masses and can be dispensed with if push comes to shove.

It is, in our opinion, only a mass of working people who are central to the economy who can hope to effectively begin to confront this ruling class which is not just national, but has global connections. The reality is that, using religion, the media and the NGOs, imperialism has thoroughly indoctrinated and ambushed the people. This mass (proletariat) must be organized, politicized and mobilized with an experience of self-reliance (soviets), loyalty to a trusted leadership; a conviction that a new world is possible and a vision of how it will look. Comrades from the middle class whose left/socialist credentials are beyond dispute should join them and provide the intellectual, ideological and technological in-put.

We italicise the terms *proletariat* and *soviets* because it is clear that a century or so later, while the main principles and strategies for a revolutionary transformation of society laid down by Marx, Engels, Lenin and Mao remain relevant, the methods and analyses adopted by the revolutionaries of the USSR or China are not always applicable today. Capitalism's neo-liberal project by its very nature creates dissent, but dissent on its own does not lead to revolutionary change. People's uprisings in Africa and elsewhere in the last decade have been truly inspiring but to date have been stalemated by the counter-revolution.

Today's revolutionaries need to study theory, adapt it to our socio-politico-economic realities and devise new methods of struggle to break through the exploitative system we live in. We have much to learn from left colleagues and movements in South Africa, Nigeria, Zimbabwe, Tanzania, Sudan and North Africa. We, middle class activists, must move away from rhetoric. We have much to learn from politicized workers with regard to this exploitation; as well as engage with basic humanity, communal organizing, solidarity and commitment. It is no easy task for us to win the necessary trust and acceptance without which we will remain 'toothless bulldogs'.

It is only by engaging in protests in support of the Constitution or Judiciary or against corruption, police brutality, evictions, land grabs, domestic violence and so much else that we can forge intra class relationships, build solidarity with working people, share our ideas and win over the sympathetic/empathetic elements in the government and the religious sector. Of course, these protests are reformist but they must be seen as the means to achieving the revolutionary goal of forming the post-capitalist state.

1. Given the huge advances in technology, weaponry, surveillance, AI, etc. the previous methods of confrontation and armed struggle are no longer as applicable. Globally there is a move to support community and grass-root populations which seek to minimize victimization by the capitalist system by becoming more self-reliant and self-sustaining, strengthen their class organisations and ensure the full participation of women with the long-term view of building international alliances to break down the walls of global capitalism. For an inspiring read visit .

A word about the role of women. Just as racism is a vital pillar of capitalism, even more universal is the ideology of patriarchy; and just as we support the campaigns against racism, patriarchy needs to be challenged NOW. The family and its exploitation is the kingpin of this economic system, socializing the family and liberating women is a key task if we are to enlist the full participation of half of the population, and lay the building blocks of a new society. Women activists are already making their presence felt in the radical/revolutionary movements across the world. In Africa, this is evidenced in Egypt, Algeria, Sudan, South Africa, Nigeria and here in Kenya too. But without women in leadership and decision-making positions in our organisations, socialization of the family will not be achieved.

There are no short cuts to building this new world – it is a journey of 'a hundred miles'. Demonstrations and marches and reliving our past patriotic history are only the first steps; we have a long way to go. We are on the right side of history but we are few in number and we must not underestimate the power of the forces against us. Nor must we dissipate our energies and our resources wantonly. To participate in parliamentary elections at this time when we have neither the required organizational support nor the mass base is an exercise in futility and a waste of time and resources. And it has the added undesirable result of once again reaffirming the importance of elections in the people's psyche.

Endnotes

1. Awaaz Voices, (2021). I've come to learn that if you want to change the world, you must change people, and in this music has great power. (online) Available at https://www.awaazmagazine.com/volume-18/issue-2/special-feature/shyam-shah (Accessed: 1 September 2021).

2. Blog of the APA, (2020). From Durban to the World. (online) Available at https://blog.apaonline.org/2020/12/25/from-durban-to-the-world/ (Accessed: 1 September 2021).

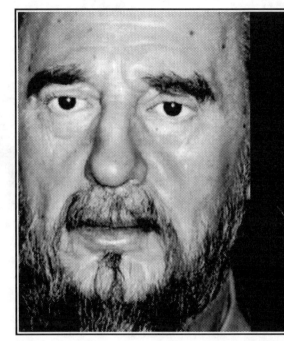

The revolution has no time for elections. There is no more democratic government in Latin America than the revolutionary government.

— *Fidel Castro* —

AZ QUOTES

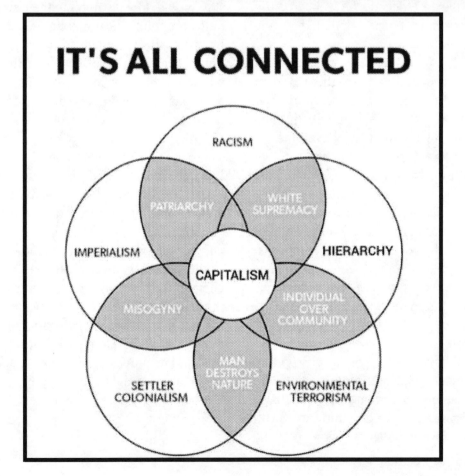

On the Education of the People

Bill David

The last two decades have witnessed an unprecedented (one can even say, obsessive), offensive against the ideas of socialism on a world scale. The collapse of the Soviet Union and it's bureaucratically planned system, alongside it's Eastern European satellites, was held up as definite proof of the unworkability of Socialism.

In fact, some, like the American Francis Fukayama, were as bold as to pronounce not just the death of Communism but also "the end of the History".

It behoves the vanguard for/of socialism to mount a defence. But many such efforts have proved counterproductive in the past. They were carried out in the realms of theory and above the mundane everyday realities of the lives of people. They thus failed to find any resonance with working people.

The defence of socialism and socialist ideas need not be made through long-winded academic discourses. Any such attempts would appear to be mere apologetics. Indeed, most of those which have appeared have been too stringent, too defensive and even shrill in trying to counter the detractors.

Marxism has withstood centuries of attacks, misinterpretation, misappropriation, misapplication, and distortion. Marx, Engels, Lenin, Trotsky, and others had long predicted such eventualities.

But did socialism really die? Was there such a conclusive proof of it unviability? Socialism never died nor is it unviable. Why?

The main reason for this is the living reality of socialist ideas. Whether in the ghettos of South Africa, the favellas of Brazil or the sweat shops of China, the life conditions of the people are a testament to the unworkability of capitalism.

It's heartening that *The Kenya Socialist* should appear at this critical time, when capitalism appears to be in its death throes, it needs concerted efforts to push it off the cliff.

The task of educating the masses can't be more urgent as in the present.

With the prevailing political illiteracy, fostered by the ruling class, it's imperative that counter arguments/offensives should be made.

Despite the glaring socioeconomic and political iniquities in the society, and the people's receptive mood for change, the ruling class usually channels such steam into harmless parliamentary, electoral activities. They disarm the people and drown their felt grievances in superficial changes involving parties or individuals.

The ruling class never addresses the need for a change of the system – capitalism itself. Doing so would be suicidal for it as a class.

The ruling class therefore is never interested in the real education of the masses. They would not have an enlightened, informed and rational citizenry. Such a people pose a danger, not just to the existing regimes, but also those aspiring to replace them.

The people remain the poorer for it.

Let's keep up the good work.

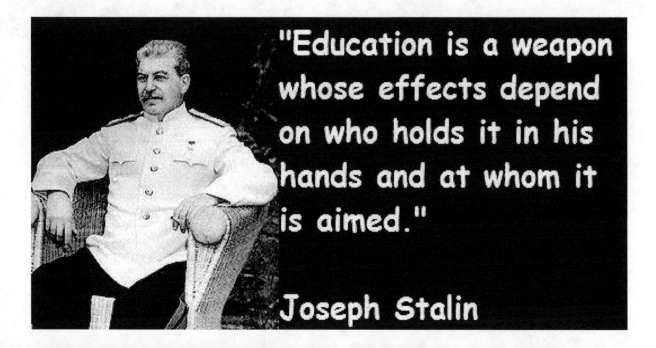

Kenya: Repression and Resistance: From Colony to Neo-Colony, 1948-1990. Part 2: Illustration

Issue No. 3 of The Kenya Socialist carried the first part of the above article by Shiraz Durrani and Kimani Waweru. The article which appeared in the Palgrave Encyclopedia of Imperialism and Anti-Imperialism ((2nd ed., 2021) did not contain illustrations prepared with the article. This issue of TKS reproduces some of the illustrations from that file. Ukombozi Library has the full paper collection of the original documents. There is a now an attempt by Vita Books, Ukombozi Library and History254 to digitise these and other material in Kenya Resistance, under the title, the Kenya Resistance Archives. Contact the Editors or History254 for further details about the digitisation Project.

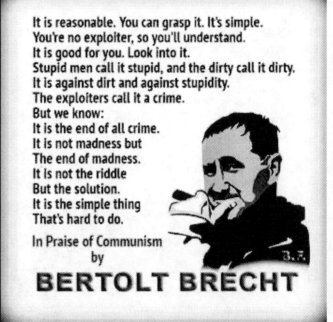

People Resist

Countdown to Freedom. (Africa Events 1990)

Saba Saba resistance (Africa Events 1990)

Saba Saba resistors (Africa Events, 1990)

Police Disperse Protesters (1992)
Police dispersing Kenyans protesting in Uhuru Park, Freedom Corner in Nairobi calling for the release of political prisoners. March 1992. (Photo: Khamisi Ramdhan)

University of Nairobi students demonstrate (1992) *(Photo: Nation)*

Molo residents demonstrate (1992) *Photo: Nation*

ORGANISED RESISTANCE
December Twelve Movement (DTM

InDependent Kenya. (1982) front cover

Political Economy ● Africa
INDEPENDENT KENYA

Independent Kenya is a devastating exposé of Kenya during the 20 years since Independence. In vigorous language and with lots of concrete examples, the authors tell the real story of Kenya today — the extent of corruption, the enrichment of certain individuals, the suppression of all opposition. They also analyse the country's distorted economy, polarised class structure, and cultural dependency on the West. The book ends with an outline of the various political possibilities for the future, the authors arguing that the struggle for scientific socialism, while inevitable if the Kenyan people are to free themselves from poverty and repression, can only result from a lengthy and difficult period of political organization and struggle.

The authors are a group of Kenyans from various parts of the country. They have had to remain anonymous because they are still living there. The text had already circulated quite extensively in mimeographed form before political activity became almost impossible with the brutal repression that followed the air force rising in late 1982.

ISBN Hb 0 86232 078 X
      Pb 0 86232 079 8

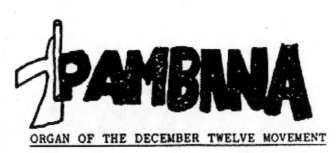

ORGAN OF THE DECEMBER TWELVE MOVEMENT

MEI/MAY 1982   Na./No. 1

MSIMAMO WETU

Wakenya tumehainiwa, na mapinduzi tuliyoya- mwagia damu nyingi ili kuikomboa inchi yetu sasa yamepotoshwa na kunajisiwa.

Leo, baada ya miaka 22 tangu chama cha KANU kiundwe, na miaka 20 tangu tudanganywe kwa uhuru uongo, hali ya maisha yetu imezoroteka kabisa kabisa. Hawa viongozi wetu majambazi wamelitup- ilia mbali jukumu lao la kuyaongoza maisha yetu na wametutendea jinai kubwa hata kuliko ile ya wakoloni: wametunyamazisha kwa nguvu, na wametu- pokonya haki yetu ya kushiriki katika harakati za taifa letu. Haki zetu za kujieleza, za kuse- ma tunalotaka, za kukutana tunapotaka zote zime- tupwa jaani.

KANU na serikali yake wameuchafua uchumi wetu, wameufuja ushirikiano wetu, wameleta mafa- rakano baina yetu huku wakituibia na kurundika pesa nyingi na miliki ya taifa. Wamewapa wabe- beru inchi yetu ili waifanye chombo cha siasa zao za kutudhulumu na kambi ya majeshi yao ya kutunyanyasa. Na hatia hizi zote za jinai zime- tendwa eti kwa jina la "maendeleo" na porojo la Nyayo la "mapenzi, amani na umoja".

Huu, ndugu zetu SI uhuru.

Huu ni ubeberu, ukoloni mambo-leo wa hali mbovu kabisa. Wakenya wamepigana vita vingi ha- po zamani ili waitoe Kenya katika utumwa wa aina hii. Hawakupigana ili maisha yao yazidi kuzoro- teka! Kweli tulifanya makosa, makosa ya kutowa- ng'oa wasaliti kati yetu, makosa makubwa ya ku- waacha vibaraka vya wakoloni kuungana na kutu-

OUR STAND

Kenyans have been massively betrayed. The revolution we launched with blood has been arrested and derailed.

Today, more than 22 years after KANU was formed and almost 20 years after a fake indepe- ndence was negotiated, the broad masses of Kenya are materially and politically worse off than ever before. The criminally corrupt rul- ing clique, sanctioned by KANU has isolated itself from the concerns of our daily life and has committed a crime among many others, more brutal than any that British colonialism ever did: they have silenced all opposition and deprived us, forcibly and otherwise, of the very right to participate in Kenya's national affairs. The sacred rights of expression and association have been cast aside.

KANU and its government have disorganized all spheres of economic production, have scat- tered all communal efforts at organization, have sowed unprincipled discord and enmity among our peoples, and have looted unspeakable sums of money and national wealth. They have finally given our entire country over to U.S. imperialism to use as a political and military base. All these crimes have been wrought in the name of "progress and prosperity" and inane smatterings of "love, peace and unity".

This is NOT independence.

This is neo-colonialism in its worst form. Kenyans have fought many battles in order to

1

Pambana No. 1 (May 1982)

PAMBANA

ORGAN OF THE DECEMBER TWELVE MOVEMENT

JULY 1983   No. 2

From the first issue of PAMBANA . . .

1. Firmly opposes the robbery of our national resources and wealth by imperialist interests be they multinational corporations, banks or foreign governments. Kenyan wealth and labour must benefit Kenyans only.

2. Condemns in the strongest of terms the criminally corrupt and traitorous band of thieves who govern this country and who have allied themselves with US imperialism to keep us perpetually down.

3. Is totally opposed to the presence on Kenyan soil of US and any other military bases.

4. Supports all genuine, democratic and liberation movements fighting for people's self-determination in and outside Kenya.

KENYA: THE STRUGGLE CONTINUES

EDITORIAL

PAMBANA STANDS FOR UNITY

When the first issue of PAMBANA came out in May 1982, the people of Kenya and all freedom-loving people of the world received it with great joy. It filled Kenyans with hope and great expectations. It made them see that it was possible to change the prevailing oppressive conditions and create a better life for all Kenyans. This is what they had always looked forward to—an organ which would unite the poor and the exploited against the Kenyan ruling class and their foreign masters. Such a unity is what PAMBANA stands for.

PAMBANA united the poor and all those who love freedom and democracy; it united the workers and peasants all over Kenya; it united all the patriots in the civil service, the police and the army; it united students, teachers, lawyers, journalists, doctors, nurses, secretaries, mechanics, shop assistants and office workers. They all hailed PAMBANA's call for a relentless struggle against imperialism.

KANU IN THE SERVICE OF EURO-AMERICAN IMPERIALISM

Here in Kenya, the oppression of people is systematically done on behalf of Euro-American imperialists by the KANU-led ruling class. The imperialists milk our country dry while their watchdogs, the KANU-led regime rule over us like gods. These "gods" felt threatened by the unity and consciousness created by PAMBANA and they responded by detentions without trial, imprisonment on trumped-up charges and indiscriminate torture of Kenyans. Anyone who dared to speak for democracy and constitutional rights was thrown into detention. Journalists, teachers, lawyers, workers, students, peasants were harassed mercilessly. They underwent brutal police interrogations. They were put into custody and prison because they dared to demand their democratic rights, they dared oppose a one-party dictatorship and what is more they dared oppose the granting of military bases to the United States of America.

The Kenyan comprador ruling clique cunningly exploited the attempted coup of August 1, 1982 to kill thousands of innocent people, especially our young patriotic Kenyans, and to cow people into accepting the regime's murderous rule. The regime used the occasion to silence the voices of patriotic youth who sincerely believed in changes that would lead to democracy and socialism.

For three continuous months (August,

September and October 1982), the ruling clique and their army used guns to instil fear amongst the people. Moi's soldiers raped our women; robbed Kenyan peasants and workers of their property; snatched clothes, shoes, watches and radios from people travelling in 'matatus'; went into people's homes and took anything they wanted from innocent and unarmed people. They took the little that the workers had saved through showed they were the enemy of the people. They behaved like the U.S. soldiers in Vietnam; the elders said that they behaved like the colonial British 'johnies' during the British imposed State of Emergency. The army, trained and groomed by the Americans and the British, was mercilessly used against the people. We are totally opposed to these murderous brutes, going under the name of Kenya Armed Forces. We oppose an army which guards the property of foreign capitalists and their comprador agents. But these soldiers are children of peasants and workers, and so when they use force against the people of their own class, it is like raping their own mothers.

There is no difference between the leaders of KANU and the leaders of neo-colonial regimes like Chile, El-Salvador, Guatemala, Honduras, Indonesia, Philippines, Pakistan, etc. These countries have military comprador regimes created by US imperialists to perpetuate the exploitation of workers and rob the wealth of these countries. In these countries, the struggle of

peasants and workers to bring about democracy and socialism has reached a high stage. These people will surely defeat the fascist foreign-supported regimes as the peoples of Vietnam, Kampuchea and Nicaragua have done.

On August 1, 1982 the people of Kenya expressed their deep-rooted desire to change their condition of daily oppression by their attitude to the coup attempt. Thousands of people all over the country celebrated the announcement of the coup because it showed that it was possible to become free from oppression by the police, the administration, city council 'askaris', and the whole

government machinery administered by corrupt and unpatriotic government officials; that it was possible to free themselves from the oppression of foreign lawyers, and some Kenyan lawyers too, who are the willing tools of the 'mbwa kali' class. For thousands of hungry and unemployed, any change that would modify the prevailing conditions was welcome. This explains their enthusiastic reception of the news of the August attempted coup.

MILITARY-BACKED KANU REGIME INTENSIFIES REPRESSION

The KANU government, with its army, attacked and tortured unarmed people. Thus the government and the comprador-ruling class, exposed their true face as the enemy of the people. The authoritarian regime of Moi must repress all opposition with brutal force. How shall we ever forget the threats, the harassment and the torture against us by the Moi-Mulinge regime in 1982?

The military-backed KANU regime has continued the oppression, this time under the guise of defending and upholding the constitution. Yet most Kenyans know the regime has no respect even for its own laws and constitution as shown by the kangaroo military courts, the students' show trials and many political jailings and detentions. Biased judgements against workers in trade union disputes with foreign-owned companies are the order of the day, while cases of corruption involving directors, managers and senior civil servants are often dropped. Foreign judges (European, US and British Asian) are highly paid rubber stamps. Unpatriotic Kenyan (African & Asian)

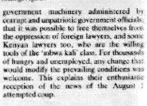

The harassment and the torture against us by the Moi-Mulinge regime.

MWAKENYA

Mwakenya: Draft Minimum Programme (1987)

Register of Resistance 1986 (1987)

One Kenya, many nationalities (1987) Mwakenya DMP

FIELD MARSHAL BAIMUNGI

PIO GAMA PINTO

KIMATHI WA WACIURI

FIELD MARSHAL MWARIAMA N'KIRIGUA

FIELD MARSHAL MUTHONI

GENERAL TANGANYIKA MURIUKI KAMOTHO

MAKHAN SINGH

A MAU MAU GENERAL INSPECTS TROOPS IN THE FOREST

Heroes & Heroines of our Struggle Mwakenya (Mwakenya DMP, 1987)

Mwakenya's Democracy Plank (1991)

Mpango wa Demokrasia wa Mwakenya (1991)

Msimamo wa Mwakenya (1992)

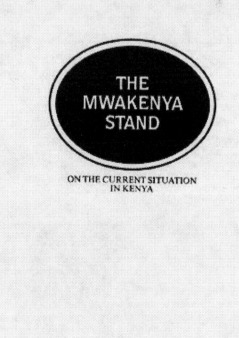

The Mwakenya Stand (1992)

Umoja

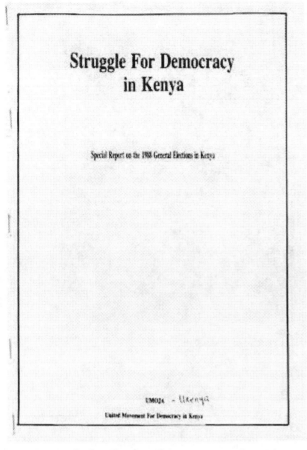

Struggle for democracy in Kenya (1988)

Moi's Reign of Terror (MRT, 1989)

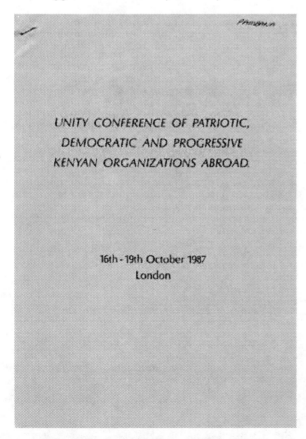

Umoja Unity Conference. London. October 1987

Habari za Umoja No. 1 1989
Umoja Statements (1987-1989)
Umoja Unity Conference

UNITY CONFERENCE OF PATRIOTIC, DEMOCRATIC AND PROGRESSIVE KENYAN ORGANIZATIONS ABROAD.

16th-19th October 1987
London

NB: This is a draft copy for discussion.

Habari za Umoja No. 1 1989
Umoja Statements (1987-1989)
Umoja Unity Conference

Comitee for the Release of Political Prisoner in Kenya, London

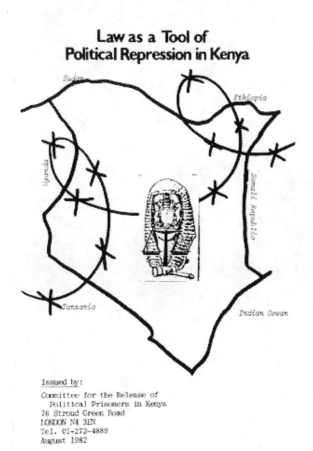

Release Political Prisoners in Kenya

APRIL 1984 ISSUE 3

KENYA NEWS

BULLETIN OF THE COMMITTEE FOR THE RELEASE OF POLITICAL PRISONERS IN KENYA

STOP THIS MASSACRE

The barbaric attack by the Kenyan security forces on defenceless citizens in the Northeast Province killed more than 1,000 people. It is a fresh reminder that the Kenyan government's policy of rule by repression and terror applies to all Kenyans. The tragedy of the northeast's five day massacre was the inevitable climax to the colonial and neo-colonial regimes' treatment of all northern Kenya as a restricted area where normal laws do not apply.

For years the northeast's only use to the government has been as a playground for privileged western hunters often brought into the country with no proper formalities. But under President Moi's government the vast desert area has come to be even more prized—as a key area for the foreign military who are allowed to use Kenya for their own geopolitical ends. Wajir is the location of the Israeli-built airforce base.

The northern province of Kenya has been under a State of Emergency during both the British colonial-settler regime and the neo-colonial regimes of Kenyatta and Moi. Even today, Kenyans living outside the province need a special permit from the government to visit the area and the people of northern Kenya are treated by the central government as foreigners in their own country. In fact the area from Wajir to Turkana is similar to one vast prison, where the armed forces are a law unto themselves. Under the pretext of combating secessionist *shiftas* the area has been used by the security forces for tactical experiments in mass torture and killings.

Since independence most of the provincial and district commissioners posted to the area (like Eliud Mahihu and Benson Kaaria) were administering the Emergency Laws imposed by the British to repress the Kenya Land and Freedom Army (MAU MAU). What they and the military learned in torturing Mau Mau freedom fighters has been systematically used in northern Kenya. And the methods further developed have later been used in other parts of the country. For example, following the attempted coup of August 1982 which had been crushed within hours an estimated 2,000 people were killed by the security forces.

The people of the north have been neglected by successive colonial and neo-colonial governments. The areas have been abandoned to the care of foreigners—Italian, Irish and US missionaries—or donor agencies from the Scandinavian countries. Since the area is restricted, news of what is happening very rarely comes out for the attention of the world except for the occasional dissenting voice of some of the missionaries—and on this occasion three brave Kenyans, two members of parliament and a councillor.

We appeal to the world to bring pressure on the Kenyan government to stop the barbarity and excesses of the security forces responsible for this massacre of innocent and defenceless Kenyans.

NEW DETENTIONS

In January at least 11 people in Northwest Province were detained under emergency legislation dating back to the colonial period and which allows the local administration draconian powers of detention, restriction and deportation from the area. The District Commissioner can detain anyone for 28 days and can extend the detention order indefinitely.

Northern Kenyan detainees are not normally gazetted and some have been held for many years. Six of those detained, all from Mandera, were released after 28 days. The remaining five, from Wajir, were released in March. They include a former Assistant Minister, Abdisirat Khalif Mohamed, the Chairman of Wajir County Council, Mohamed Noor, and a former Councillor, Ahmed Elmi.

MASSACRE IN WAJIR

The purpose of this Press release is to enlighten the Nation and our beloved government about the nature and magnitude of the mass killings in cold blood of innocent, lawful and law abiding citizens between the 10th and 14th February, 1984 in Wajir District.

On the 10th February, 1984 army personnel and the Kenya Police in Wajir District rounded up men of the Degodia Tribe in the district and put them in a camp nine miles away from Wajir township. Over 5,000 (five thousand) men were eventually held up. These people included ordinary *wananchi*, businessmen, prominent religious leaders and civil servants, were stripped naked and forced to lie on their bellies. Those who resisted to go nude were shot on the spot as the rest were denied water and food by the security personnel who enforced the order for the people to continue lying down on their bellies under severe rays of the hot sun. They were subjected to torture by the security personnel who continued to beat them. As days continued severity of the atrocities by the security personnel inflicted upon the people included clubbing some of the people to death and some others were burnt alive.

This Hitlerite process of human elimination continued for five consecutive days. I was in Wajir as all this happened and later on 15th February, I along with other missionaries went out to attend to the survivors who were transported by the security personnel far away from anywhere they could receive assistance to save their lives. As we searched for the survivors we also realised that most people who died in the camp were being transported and dumped far away in the countryside apparently for cover up.

We managed to get some of the survivors and brought them to Wajir township for medical care. The authorities in Wajir have however persistently denied relatives of the dead to retrieve their dead from the countryside for burial.

The over 5,000 men who were concentrated at Wagalla airstrip were all snatched of their identification cards by the security personnel and it is believed they have been destroyed. Only a thorough and fair investigation will establish the exact numbers of the death toll, however as of now the number of the confirmed dead is over 300.

These include 26 civil servants, prominent businessmen and religious leaders. Over 1,000 men who were among the people held at the camp are also missing and are believed to be dead.

As men of the Degodia tribe were rounded up on the 10th February, the security forces burnt down houses of the tribesmen to ashes both in Wajir township and at various divisions. Thousands of families who were thus rendered homeless instantly now need immediate shelter. As many of the guardians of these homeless families were killed they also need food aid. I am among those whose houses were burnt.

The purpose of this press release is to appeal to our beloved government to institute impartial and fair investigations to establish the awful truth of the situation. Yet no commission, however impartial it may be, can unearth the truth as long as the perpetrators of these heinous crimes are still there. It is therefore necessary that these people should be removed in order to create acceptable conditions for fair and just inquiry.

Last but not the least I wish to take this opportunity to register our unswerving loyalty to our beloved President His Excellency Hon. Daniel arap Moi in person, the Party and the Government.

Signed:
CLLR. SUGAL A. UNSHUR
COUNCILLOR WAJIR TOWNSHIPS

Kenya News No. 3 (1984)

MAY 1985 ISSUE 5

KENYA NEWS

BULLETIN OF THE COMMITTEE FOR THE RELEASE OF POLITICAL PRISONERS IN KENYA

SUNDAY BLOODY SUNDAY

Once again a democratic gathering of students of the University of Nairobi has been met with truncheons, teargas and bullets. The calculated brutality has yet again exposed the repressive and anti-people character of the Moi regime.

Twelve students including a pregnant woman were bludgeoned to death. More than 150 others were admitted to hospital. The death toll could rise as at least thirty are known to have been critically injured. To cover up the extent of the carnage, the regime has once again closed the University.

Even before the Sunday massacre of 10th February, the University which reopened in October 1983 after 14 months of another closure had ceased to function like a normal seat of learning and research. Undercover policemen were planted among the students to spy on the entire University community. The President himself increasingly attempted to take personal control of the conduct of students and staff. The regime even tried to foist a state-approved leadership on the students. But the students would seem to have committed the "crime" of having their own minds and opting for a popularly approved leadership. This leadership around Julius Mwandawiro MGHANGA wanted to form a National Union of Students of Kenya (NUSKE). The students called for the release of their 10 colleagues imprisoned since 1982. They questioned why their colleagues were still locked in maximum security prisons on framed charges while the President had shown an indecent hurry to pardon Charles Njonjo found "guilty" by the government's own Commission of Inquiry of plotting to overthrow the regime in 1982. The students exposed cases of corrupt admissions to the University meaning backdoor admissions of favourites by a Presidential directive. These democratic demands and legitimate questions were met with police truncheons and bullets on the bloody Sunday.

Since the present regime assumed power in 1978 and particularly after 1980 when it had given USA military "facilities" it has been characterised by an almost pathological hostility to democratic activities and organisations.

In 1982 the regime legislated a one-party state with KANU as the sole political party, after only five minutes "debate" in parliament. Prior to this, it had banned all social welfare organisations; the Kenya Civil Servants Union; the University Academic Staff Union; and cracked down on all national and patriotic cultural activities particularly theatre. Even the church has not been spared. Church services have been under police surveillance, with certain clergymen coming under intense government harassment. Trade Unions have been muzzled. Workers strikes and demands for higher wages to meet the ever spiralling food prices have been answered with police baton charges and presidentially directed dismissals. The recent dismissals of striking bank workers is only one example among many. The University has borne the brunt of Moi's repressive measures. University lecturers have been detained without trial or else imprisoned on trumped up charges. The students have had their classes interrupted by the riot police or constant closures. And now after the bloody Sunday of 10th February 1985, at least five students including Julius Mwandawiro MGHANGA are facing yet another political trial which could lead to long jail sentences.

Patrick Shaw and riot squad

But the regime's hostility to democratic practices has been matched by the even more sinister and extreme indifference to Kenyan lives. The senseless massacre of more than 1000 people in Wajir and a similar number in Pokot in 1983 are the better known cases. But there are others; and the reports of a mass grave of more than 40 bodies in Nakuru are very alarming. Most of these atrocities were happening in "remote" areas where the regime has total control over the flow of information. Now it has happened in the capital, at the citadel of knowledge in what was by all accounts a peaceful prayer meeting on a Sunday. Ironically it was an interdenominational prayer for peace.

The Moi regime hopes to hoodwink the nation and the world by resorting to a by now familiar ploy; the claims that ALL the internal discontent, dissent and opposition are foreign instigated.

All those who love democracy, peace and religious tolerance and all those who sincerely uphold the Universal declaration of human rights must not buy the regime's lies and its attempts to shift the blame from itself. Instead they should answer the lies by sending letters of protest and concern to the Kenyan authorities.

The Committee for the Release of Political Prisoners in Kenya condemns the latest cold blooded murder of innocent students and condemns the perennial use of state violence against the people of Kenya.

We ask all those individuals and organisations who have been calling for the release of all political prisoners including lecturer Maina wa KINYATTI and the 10 students imprisoned since 1982 to yet again call upon the regime to release Julius Mwandawiro MGHANGA and the other students facing trials after the Bloody Sunday; to reopen the University; and to keep the police away from the classrooms, libraries and student halls of residence.

Kenya News No. 5 (1995)

JUNE 1985 ISSUE 6

KENYA NEWS

BULLETIN OF THE COMMITTEE FOR THE RELEASE OF POLITICAL
PRISONERS IN KENYA

THE KENYAN WOMAN:
A DECADE OF OPPRESSION

The United Nations Decade for Women launched in Mexico City in 1975 and now coming to an end in Nairobi in July 1985 was intended to improve the conditions of women worldwide.

But for the Kenyan peasant and working woman and indeed for the society as a whole, it has been a decade of increased repression, general harassment and police brutality. The woman peasant and worker has borne the brunt of the massive economic, political and cultural repression in the country. The decade has seen the kenyan peasant woman continue to be a beast of burden without any rights and security of food, housing and adequate clothing. She is the first to produce food: the last to eat it. The worst jobs and lowest wages in coffee, tea, sisal plantations and in factories are reserved for her. Women trying to eke a living by selling vegetables in Nairobi live under daily terror from police and municipal askaris. The city has to be kept clean and tidt for tourists and delegates of international conferences. Many women have been hounded into the ever increasing prison population. Others have been mauled to death by Alsation guard dogs at Kenya Canners, Thika, a subsidiary of the multinational corporation, Del Monte.

Thus whether in US-led multi-nationals; US-sponsored population programmes; US military facilities; or indeed at her home, place of work and in the streets, the peasant/worker woman has been the main victim in neo-colonial Kenya. Perhaps the most scandalous have been the effect of popula-

tion control measures and the impact of US military bases on the Kenyan woman.

The population control programme in Kenya is part of the cover-up for the massive corruption and economic mismanagement, the drainage of Kenya's wealth to western countries and all the policies which together have created a country of "ten millionaires and ten million beggars." The resultant poverty and misery of the masses have been blamed on the fertility of Kenyan woman. "Breeding like rabbits", "too many mouths to feed", are some of the phrases in the official jargon of abuse and contempt for the people, as if it is not the peasant woman who produces the very food and crops the regime sends abroad.

Therefore no experimentation however risky, no method however controversial, and no drugs however unsafe have been spared the Kenyan woman.

The Kenya government was among the earliest to accept and promote the widespread use of Depo-provera on Kenyan women. The high-oestrogen pills and the Dalkon Shield IUD, which has been the cause of numerous cases of serious uterine infections and even deaths in the US and Britain, are used widely in Kenya.

Indeed, over the decade Kenya has become a major dumping ground for defective medical devices, lethal drugs, known carcinogens, toxic pesticides, cosmetics containing corrosive

continued on page 4

Kenya News No. 6 (1985)

AUGUST 1986 ISSUE 7

KENYA NEWS

BULLETIN OF THE COMMITTEE FOR THE RELEASE OF POLITICAL PRISONERS IN KENYA

STATE OF EMERGENCY

By a special correspondent, Nairobi, August, 1986

An eerie chill of public silence has descended over the nation as the Moi regime continues the severest crackdown in post-independent Kenya. Hundreds have been imprisoned in the last few months for suspected or openly expressed "dissident" views, but the escalating arrests have done little to stem the tide of *Mwakenya* penetration into even the most secure national institutions. The latest example of the length of the underground movement was its ability to place a new leaflet in the pigeonhole of every Member of Parliament in the National Assembly building.

The security forces inability to root out the extensive underground network is forcing them to employ increasingly arbitrary and unlawful methods. Detentions without trial, required by law to be gazetted within 14 days of arrest, are being announced many months late, while many other political prisoners are being held incommunicado with no official word of whether they are indeed in police custody. Reflecting this blatantly anti-legal tendency - and the desperation of the intelligence services - was the recent arrest and mistreatment of Salim Lone, the former editor of *Viva* magazine who is now a United Nations official in New York. This step, an explicit violation of international protocols the Kenya government has signed, was the latest expression of the authorities' frustration to make headway against *Mwakenya*, and their willingness to risk international protests in their desperate attempts to seek out and silence those suspected of anti-Nyayo views.

The President himself revealed how desperate his regime was over the question of *Mwakenya* when he announced in July that Kanu officials would be held accountable if dissident elements were uncovered in their districts. So totally is the regime obsessed with the fear of the underground movement that Kenya insisted (at the July regional heads of state meeting in Nairobi) on placing the question of dissidents who flee to neighbouring countries at the top of the summit agenda. The 7 country meeting of Kenya, Sudan, Uganda, Tanzania, Rwanda, Burundi, and Zaire - obliged the hosts by agreeing to much closer co-operation and exchange of information in this area.

In this environment of intimidation - and reported prison tortures - the mood in every national institution is one of fear.

Even Cabinet ministers stay away now from commenting on any but the most clear-cut issues, and the press has never been more docile in the country's history. But the fear is greatest at the University, with many lecturers and students in prison and even the most middle-of-the-road teachers under suspicion and surveillance. Most lecturers have therefore abandoned their responsibility of "teaching" their students, in fear of their views being misrepresented by the network of informers who attend classes.

continued on page 2

HELP CLOSE MOI'S TORTURE CHAMBERS

EDITORIAL

Since 1982 *Kenya News* has been exposing different aspects of the barbarous character of the Moi regime in Kenya. Following the massacres in Wajir and Pokot in 1983 and 1984, the killings of students on Bloody Sunday in February 1985, the executions of political prisoners during the Women's Conference in Nairobi in 1985, the regime has begun the Systematic torture of those it suspects of membership in or sympathetic to the resistance movement in the country.

Nearly all the political prisoners arrested or detained since January this year were kept incommunicado for at least a month. Those who were mutilated by the beatings, water torture and other methods used routinely in the underground chambers (of torture) of Nyayo House on Kenyatta Avenue have been detained or have disappeared. The Kenya security services, trained by the U.S., Israel and Britain, have developed a crude brutality reminiscent of that used under U.S. backed dictatorships in Latin America. Many of those who have appeared in court had signed confessions which were obtained under torture. Many denounced their torturers to their faces in the court room, despite attempts to gag them by the prosecution and even the judiciary.

Again, as in Latin America, the judiciary has become the personal tool of the Head of State in enforcing repression. The President has only to telephone the Chief Magistrate to ensure convictions and long sentences for anyone identified through his paranoia as a threat. Magistrates who have attempted to demonstrate a measure of independence have been demoted.

As usual, the prime targets have been intellectuals, students and teachers, but the net has gone wider than ever in recent months with many workers and peasants arrested for acts of resistance or for such "political crimes as reading underground papers. These are only the tips of an iceberg for names of ordinary peasants and workers rarely find their way into the newspapers except in flagrant cases where thousands are involved such as the Wajir massacre.

An indication of the extent of the repression and the regime's desperate attempts to stem resistance is the recall from retirement of Jeremiah Kierieni, and other veterans of the colonial campaign against Mau Mau in the 1950s to lead the interrogations of those suspected of being members of *Mwakenya* resistance movement.

Jeremiah Kierieni, Chief Secretary under Kenyatta and Moi, had his photo printed in the 1984 Noma Prize-winning book,

TORTURE TRADE

Flashback to KENYA NEWS of June 1985 (Issue No.6). Torture implements imported then are in full use now.

continued on page 6

Kenya News No. 7 (1986)

1

January 1989
Issue 9

KENYA NEWS

BULLETIN OF THE COMMITTEE FOR THE RELEASE OF POLITICAL PRISONERS IN KENYA

MOI'S POLICE: LICENCE TO KILL

There has been an alarming increase in the number of deaths in Kenya: in police custody, in prison, in public places and in large scale massacres by security forces. It is now internationally acknowledged that the Kenyan government has systematically violated most of the basic and fundamental human rights guaranteed by the Kenyan constitution and the International Covenant on Civil and Political Rights, to which Kenya acceded in 1972.

In the March 1987 edition of Kenya News the committee for the Release of Political Prisoners in Kenya (CRPPK) highlighted the increase in torture. The international press, as well as some governments, organisations and hundreds of individuals worldwide, have expressed concern at the increase in human rights violations in Kenya. Amnesty International has continued to issue urgent appeals for action and has recently issued an up-date of the July 1987 report, Kenya; Torture, Political Detention and Unfair Trials. To highlight the increase in torture and in particular, deaths resulting from it, the CRPPK held a 12-hour vigil for the victims of torture outside the Kenya High Commission in London on July 29, 1987. At that time about 10 people were known to have

been tortured to death in police custody. What has changed since has been the frequency of killings by government agents. With no curbs from their masters, the police have picked up people from their homes and tortured them to death; they have shot people in their homes and in the streets often on the flimsiest excuse and almost always with no provocation. The families battle for justice, but the government will not admit its responsibility, let alone compensate families. No wonder the police continue in their brutality. Moreover the killings now occur in every part of the country and affect people in all walks of life.

In the 'Dear Friend' letter of March 18, 1988, we listed 28 cases of people killed by the police. The numbers have continued to rise and while it has not been possible to obtain full details on all cases we have been able to document 92 cases between 1984 and 1988. These numbers are bound to increase with the recent Presidential 'shoot to kill' order which affects anyone living near a game park.

There have also been a number of political executions, the most notable being the killing of 12 leaders of the 1982 coup attempt on July 9 and 10, 1985. Three of those hanged had earlier been

handed back to Kenyan authorities by the Tanzanian government in an illegal swap of refugees between the two countries.

Official figures for deaths in prison (excluding executions) show that in 1979 the first year of Moi's rule 118 people died in prison. By 1985 the figure had tripled to 342. The total number of people who have died in prison between 1979 and 1985 is 1,409.

The numbers of police killings, torture victims, prison deaths, political executions and massacres all add up to more than 3,000 in only 4 years and are a clear indication of the total disregard for life that has characterised the Moi regime. Hardly a reason to spend more than £33m in celebration of his ten year rule.

The Committee for the Release of Political Prisoners in Kenya condemns the wanton disregard for human life and condemns the perennial use of state violence against people of Kenya. We ask all those individuals and organisations who have been calling for the release of the political prisoners to bring pressure to bear on the Kenyan government to stop the barbarity and excesses; of the security forces responsible for the deaths and massacres of innocent and defenceless Kenyans.

Inquest told of torture

A man told a Nakuru court yesterday that his brother claimed he had been tortured by the police before he died at the Rift Valley Provincial General Hospital.

Suspect killed

Mombasa police yesterday shot dead a man suspected to have been involved in a spate of armed robberies in the town while another suspected to be his accomplice escaped.

MAN DIES IN PRISON

Police shoot

MOI LEGALISES BRUTALITY

A constitutional amendment of August 3, 1988 increased the powers of President Moi and his police. This bill which was swiftly approved by Parliament gives Moi the power to dismiss High Court and Appeal Court judges without consulting a tribunal. The Law society strongly criticised this, stating that it " strikes at the very soul of the ability of a judge to perform his duties independently." The bill also extends from 24 hours to 14 days the period of time the police are permitted to hold 'suspects' without charge. Given the dismal record of the police in torturing and murdering suspects, this constitutional change is likely to lead to an increase in abuse of human and democratic rights.

In addition, those lawyers who have been willing to defend political detainees face new difficulties: all lawyers will now have to obtain a license, which can be removed by a Provincial Commissioner, a presidential appointee. When lawyers asked for discussion with the President, this was rejected and instead a commission appointed to investigate firms which have taken the cases of political detainees. A further new bill will amend the Advocates Act so that it will be in the discretion of the Attorney General instead of the Law Society to admit advocates to the High Court.

Kenyan torture **Murder**

2 more suspects shot dead by police

Two suspected robbers were shot dead by police yesterday after a chase through residential areas in Eldoret.

...nned down

Reports said the two were trying to remove the engine from a Government Toyota Hilux pick-up at the District Officer's yard at Ruringu at about 9.45 p.m. The

...ng those shot

Mrs. Mary Wangari Mwangi, 22, is an ex-student of the Uni-

Kenya News No. 9 (1989)

Cultural Resistance
MauMau

To remain united, the Mau Mau fighters sang many freedom songs.

We shall never, never give up
Without land on which to grow food,
And without our own true freedom
In our country of Kenya!

They also sang against the "loyalists" who had joined the British and the side of the settlers:

You who sell us out are our great enemies
Look around you and look at the British
And also look at yourselves
The British are foreigners
And they will surely go back to their country
Where will you, traitors to your country, run to?

There can never be compromise with the traitors
And no mercy towards them,
For the blood of hundreds of our martyrs
Cannot be forgotten
And is crying for vengeance.

MauMau

Mau Mau Freedom Song: We shall never give up

Events, Plays & Artwork

Celebrating resistance in London

Kimathi Wachiuri by Rahim

Bildad Kaggia by Oswaggo (Sehemu ya Utungaji)

Chege Kibachia. By Oswaggo (Sehemu ya Utungaji)

Fred Kubai by Oswaggo (Sehemu ya Utungaji)

Makhan Singh by Oswaggo (Sehemu ya Utungaji)

Kipande House by Oswaggo (Sehemu ya Utungaji)

Kinjikitile- Maji Maji play in Nairobi in 1984

Kenya Uhuru. Whose Freedom? (ILRIG, 1989)

VITA BOOKS

Never Be Silent Simama Imara

LIST OF BOOKS & PRICES (VAT EXCLUSIVE)

ESSAYS ON PAN-AFRICANISM Edited by Shiraz Durrani & Noosim Naimasiah	THE KENYA SOCIALIST Edited by Shiraz Durrani & Kimani Waweru No. 3	THE STRUGGLE FOR LAND & JUSTICE IN KENYA by Ambreena Manji	ESCAPE FROM MONEYVILLE by Shiraz Durrani
2022 ISBN 978-9914-9875-6-0 Pages 271 Kshs. 2,000	2021 ISBN 9789914700893 Pages 40	2021 ISBN 978-9914-9875-8-4 Pages 208 Kshs. 2,500	2021 ISBN 9789914987508 Pages 69 Kshs. 800
NEITH ER SETTLER NOR NATIVE - The Making and Unmaking of Permanent Minorities by Mahmood Mamdani	THE KENYA SOCIALIST Edited by Shiraz Durrani & Kimani Waweru No. 2	CORPSES OF UNITY – An Anthology of Poems Edited by Nsah Mala & Mbizo Chirasha	CRIMES OF CAPITALISM IN KENYA - Press Cuttings on Moi-KANU's Reign of Terror in Kenya, 1980s-1990 Compiled by Shiraz Durrani & Kimani Waweru
2020 ISBN 9789914987546 Pages 401 Kshs. 2,200	2020 ISBN 9789914700893 Pages 26	2020 ISBN 9789966133991 Pages 105 Kshs. 1,000	2020 ISBN 9789966133113 Pages 224 Kshs. 1,500

THE KENYA SOCIALIST Edited by Shiraz Durrani & Kimani Waweru No. 1 2019 ISBN 978-9966133816 Pages 37	PIO GAMA PINTO Kenya's Unsung Martyr. 1927 - 1965 Edited by Shiraz Durrani 2018 ISBN 9789966189004 Pages 391 Kshs. 2,200.00/=	MAU MAU THE REVOLUTIONARY, ANTI-IMPERIALIST FORCE FROM KENYA: 1948-1963 by Shiraz Durrani 2018 ISBN 9789966804020 Pages 154 Kshs. 800/=	TRADE UNIONS IN KENYA'S WAR OF INDEPENDENCE by Shiraz Durrani 2018 ISBN 9789966189097 Pages 118 Kshs. 800/=
PEOPLE'S RESISTANCE TO COLONIALISM AND IMPERIALISM IN KENYA by Shiraz Durrani 2018 ISBN 9789966114525 Pages 124 Kshs. 800/=	KENYA'S WAR OF INDEPENDENCE - Mau Mau and its Legacy of Resistance to Colonialism and Imperialism, 1948-1990 by Shiraz Durrani 2018 ISBN 9789966189011 Pages 450 Kshs. 1,500/=	LIBERATING MINDS, RESTORING KENYAN HISTORY - Anti-Imperialist Resistance by Progressive South Asian Kenyans 1884-1965 by Nazmi Durrani 2017 ISBN 9789966189097 Pages 202 Kshs. 800/=	MAKHAN SINGH. A Revolutionary Kenyan Trade Unionist Edited by Shiraz Durrani 2016 ISBN 1869886135 Pages 194 Kshs. 1,200/=
PROGRESSIVE LIBRARIANSHIP Perspectives from Kenya and Britain, 1979-2010 by Shiraz Durrani 2014 ISBN 9781869886202 Pages 446 Kshs. 1,600.00/=	INFORMATION AND LIBERATION Writings on the Politics of Information and Librarianship by Shiraz Durrani 2008 ISBN 9789966189073 Pages 384 Kshs. 1,500.00/=	Publishing and Imperialism 1884-1963 by Shiraz Durrani 2008 ISBN 9789966189073 Pages 280 Kshs. 1,200.00/=	KARIMI NDUTHU: A Life in Struggle 1998 1869886127 Kshs. 300.00/=

Vita Books are available at Ukombozi Library or from the following Bookshops

● Prestige Booksellers, Mama Ngina Street next to 20th Century Cinema

● Bookstop, 2nd floor, Yaya Centre, Argwings Kodhek Road,

● **Comrades Book House-Mwimuto Shopping Centre, Lower Kabete**

● **Cheche Books & Coffee-Intertrade Africa. Lavington**

● Chania Bookshop, Moi Avenue, Tumaini House, ground floor

Available Worldwide from African Books Collective http://www.africanbookscollective.com/publishers/vitabooks

Forthcoming Books
Nazmi Durrani - Tunakataa! We Say No! Poems of Resistance
ISBN 978-9966-955-88-3

The poems depict peasant and worker resistance in Kenya in the 1980s to the oppressive Moi-KANU government. Here is the voice of people saying 'no' to capitalism and emperialism. The poems, in Kiswahili and English, are as relevant today as they were in the 1980s. They are as relevant in Kenya as they are in the rest of Africa struggling against capitalism and imperialism.

Durrani Shiraz: Key Points in the History of Kenya
1885 - 1990
ISBN 978-9914-9921-3-7

History never dies. It is embedded in people's memories when books are burnt and children are taught false histories, imagined by false historians from near and far — says the author in this book. This is the context in which Key Points in the History of Kenya, 1885-1990 is published. This, the 4th in the Kenya Resists Series from Vita Books, brings together presentations points from several conferences and meetings on the history of Kenya. It also includes short articles, some written recently, others from earlier books and articles by Shiraz Durrani. Key Points highlights many hidden facts about the history of Kenya. References are included for those who wish to explore the history further. While these books and facts are readily available in many history books, they are not easily available to all people in Kenya and in a form that meets their needs.

The book therefore aims to familiarise people with the history of Kenya. It seeks to keep people's struggles, sacrifices and history alive. The author hopes that it will be a weapon in the sense that Bertolt Brecht meant when he said: Hungry man, reach for the book: it is a weapon. That is the aim of the series, Kenya Resists too.

Durrani, Shiraz: Two Paths Ahead: The Ideological Struggle between Capitalism and Socialism in Kenya, 1960-1990

ISBN 978-9966-133-12-0

The struggle between socialism and capitalism have been long bitter and violent. Capitalism wont with the active support of USA and UK governments at the time of independence in 1963. Yet the original (1960) Kenya Africa Union (KANU) Party was in favour of socialism. It was President Jomo Kenyatta and Daniel arap Moi who used violence to suppress those advocating socialism. They used their power to massacre, assasinate, exile, imprison and disappear people and created a state of terror to silence their opponents. Capitalism became the unstated state policy. Thus imperialism won and the aims of Mau Mau were brutally suppressed. However, the desire for socialism never died. Resistance movements and opposition parties made socialism their aim, reflecting people's desire for justice, equality and empowerment.

Many studies on Kenya focus on personalities or 'tribes' or race as driver of events, ignoring the all important class and ideological positions of leaders and their Parties. Two Paths Ahead reproduces and gives a brief commentary on the documents from the opposing sides in the battles between capitalism and socialism — the original Kenya African National Union (KANU), its successor, KANU-B, and the Kenya People's Union (KPU) on economy land, labour, and social policy. It also touches upon the demands of the organisers of the 1982 Coup and traces the political stand of key leaders as proponents of capitalism or socialism. Also covered are some of the policies of the underground December Twelve Movement Mwakenya. The final section reproduces some of the documents on this ideological struggle. The book exposes the hidden hand of imperialism in the country's rush to capitalism. It fills a gap in understanding the real contradictions that divide Kenya to this day.